Jackie O. Suffers Two Husbands

and
Other Poems

by

Jessica McEntee

Finishing Line Press
Georgetown, Kentucky

Jackie O. Suffers Two Husbands

and
Other Poems

ACKNOWLEDGMENTS

Thank you to Westport Writers' Workshop, Finn, Sadie and Justin. For my
parents.

Publisher: Leah Maines
Editor: Christen Kincaid
Cover Art: Robert Knudsen, White House Photographs, John F. Kennedy
Presidential Library and Museum, Boston.
Author Photo: Justin McEntee
Cover Design: Elizabeth Maines McCleavy

Printed in the USA on acid-free paper.
Order online: www.finishinglinepress.com
also available on amazon.com

Author inquiries and mail orders:
Finishing Line Press
P. O. Box 1626
Georgetown, Kentucky 40324
U. S. A.

Table of Contents

Jackie O. Suffers Two Husbands Before She Claims Someone Else's

The dynastic one comes first, the wooer, immoderate; possessed with tapeworms of desire. Jackie—once debutante, now overripe at twenty-three—has descended from a similar breed. She thinks she can will herself into blindness—enabling her to light the room upon his arm—but her husband is amaurotic, too. He steals into bathrooms, coat rooms, wherever his white cane guides him. While still zipping his fly, he sends dispatches to the Hollywood siren, the Swedish gamine, the intern. In Dallas, he leaves her drizzled in macerated scraps. Jackie becomes librarian of his unthought thoughts.

A statue seeks a base, and Aristotle seems an ordinary man, *ugly* but intact; a cantaloupe. He's beholden to habits, schedules—yes, she soon learns: he liases with Maria Callas every Monday evening after ten. Curious how he thinks his new prize-wife will slumber while he's away, that she'll content herself with jewels, peignoirs, like a lab monkey trained to grasp at a wire doll for consolation. *Non!* She counts out hours upon raw fingertips, puttering through the hollowed abdomen of his yacht.

Jackie wears a mantle of death; her breath smells of lilies, Artistotle's daughter rages after they bury him. Maybe she *should* fold into herself, she despairs. A man named Maurice emerges—mannered, married. He brings her stalks of blue hydrangeas bound in silken cord; he praises her equine eyes. He cantillates her name. Sliding a finger down the tuck behind her knee, he whispers a reminder to them both—*breathe.*

Prelude to an Affair

The man is an infection, a waking fever dream. She hefts a box of kitty litter into her shopping cart; the granules mosaic themselves into the grayed grid of his wife's face. Searching for dried apricots, she discovers his puckered nipples. Romaine lettuce frills are the slanted hairs that drag upwards from his wrist bones, and when she reaches for a package of butter sticks, her blush troughs the dairy aisle.

Outside, she sees a slack-mouthed mailbox, opened in waiting; a frittering squirrel as it lobotomizes an acorn. By the time she reaches it, her house, too, has undergone an optical contortion. It's a pile lying supine, she gasps—it's nothing more than kindling.

In Defense of Vulnerable Men

Temptresses;
hips spangled with store-bought stars,
lashes blackened with clarified soot,
and rows of roses planted upon our cheeks.
We sweep our lids with patches
yanked from clouds and seas.

Look at us,
how we ask for it
as we loll about in public parks,
midday, airing our breasts, necks—
in full view—all while saying,
Oh, no, we only want
attention from the summer's sun.

(Does the town butcher ever declare,
I'd prefer not to sell
that pink ground chuck
I just put out on display,
bound in shimmering cellophane?)

We're ubiquitous, diffuse—
we besmirch your efforts to stay pure
for the respectable women you keep on retainer.
You escape to church;
we become the frothing thuribles that circle about.
Our incense swells the air,
while we remain remote.

You're the victims, here,
when you consider such provocations.
Why, when you think of how we tattoo ourselves
with secret codes
slipped into ankles, lower backs, divots—
aren't those implicit dares
to come hither—
and, (please!) offer us
the favor of your closest translation?

Your Power dismantled,
your delicate manhood muddled—
you insist:
we must be braille.
Fingers splayed, you lean in
to prove it.

The Poet Rimbaud Takes up Arms Dealing in Ethiopia

I've turned my great love godless,
shaking his faith from him,
coins loosed from a pocket.
He, in turn, planted a bullet
in my wrist,
a warning glyph.

Escaping Europe,
I smuggle the vessel of my body
within a wooden dhow.
Black waves demolish
my knees,
pitting prow against bone.
We land, and for twenty nights,
I camelback across the seared face
of the Somali Desert.
The sun takes its corkscrew
to my scalp;
there's not moisture enough
to spur rot's release.

At last, we alight
upon the walled city,
where end-on-end alleyways turn
my leather body as if it's
the hands of a clock.
Mosques lick me
with the nap of their tongues,
but they pronounce themselves
indifferent to my flavor.

I kidnap new lovers,
taking them between filthy,
other-lovered sheets.
Lying together, our juices set
like mortar,
sealing us thigh to thigh.
They beseech me for sweet words.
No, I refuse;
in Harar, we live our poetry.

The Confessor

His face constructed out of flames,
Davey stutters about a low-grade case
of virginity.
Surely, I hear it rattled in his voice?
My laughter turns him to water;
he slips past me,
becoming a bog beneath my thighs.

Palming his halved plum,
Stefan speaks of a fifth grade gym class,
derailed. He twitched upon the sneaker-buffed floor;
the teacher's body curved
around him, making a moat.
"A girl would never notice—or care,"
I say, hoping to turn
my words to truth.

Willis insists it's *his* cross
to bear. He rolls from me,
polishing his chestplate
with morning light.

I administer to orphaned Oliver—
all golden, backlit eyes.
He located a family somewhere placeless
within me, weeks ago,
and he returns
to make their acquaintance—
learning what he's previously
invented.

Me, I'm needless;
a waiter never stops to dine.
I've lodged my secrets
beneath the sand mound
of my breast.
That spot's never borne
the mark of any ex.

Interspecies Communication

My cat has eyes the color of absinthe, of forgetting.
During his previous life as a scamp,
he supped on cigarette butt-er sticks,
chased down by heaps of rubber bands, served al dente.
These menu items drilled holes into the pink of his stomach—
but, he overturns the dish with his left paw,
when I present him with chicken-flavored foodstuffs
made for "special needs" felines.

When I first happened upon him,
he was a darling of the underworld,
king of the thick and mystical woods,
hardly something to be *named*—
much less to petition:
Come, seat yourself upon this cat-cushion.

For weeks, I lured him,
transcribing telegraphs with meaty vittles,
so unctuous, they pooled their own shadows.
Come away, I wrote.
Leave the broken branches of your castle—
it doesn't even have serviceable plumbing.

Other, sensible creatures Peter Pipered me.
I gave up entirely on the cat.
But he miraged himself, each time I retreated.

At last, I caught him succumbing.
I litter boxed-him-in,
teaching him cursory English:
No, yes. Pet, food. Pest.

Go, earn your place here, I demanded.
Can't you hear the mice—
riotous, punch-drunk?
Tremoring behind the walls?

Now he stations himself at my glass kitchen door,
transforming his skull into a battering ram—
thundering the heartiest spot, directly
into the pane.
You'd cringe to hear the bones crunch,
the sound of Melancholia.

What? You don't want *that*,
I insist, pointing a finger
to the stream outside,
with its waist-high reeds.
Like lustrous plumage,
they shudder in the breeze.

Meanwhile, the door—
schooled on what to keep in,
and what to keep out—
holds fast.
The cat persists for an hour, sometimes more,
until, defeated, depleted,
he mewls, loud enough to stir an echo.

I hear it now as I cook,
alchemizing cow into steak.
Doesn't that blasted creature remember?

Leaving dinner as it spits from its pyre,
I tower above him.
His eyes turned to sinkholes
with desire, he beseeches—
maydaying the inkberry bush, beyond:
She doesn't understand,
calling me ungrateful, a contrarian!
Can't she see—I'm only vegetarian?

The Gut Doctor's Prescription for Acid Reflux

He reads the list of the condemned:
citrus fruits—no more snap of rind
as it breaks from flesh,
or oceanspit as the segments splay;
no pith balling like snow.
Forget about tomatoes,
my late father's fruit,
the oddness of cutting them upon a board,
how they roll in protest,
heads shaking 'innocent' upon the guillotine.
And, while you're at it,
delete the resistance of their skin
before it evanesces,
how the pap beneath
weeps seed-tears.
I should pretend I never met onions or garl-
Stop! I protest,
but he continues,
calling my flowers weeds.
Avoid wine
the way you would an illicit lover,
he who slips in and out of your mouth,
but only for a spell.
Chocolate. He sneaks this in,
before attacking coffee—
yes, the grind,
that elemental smell,
the birdsong of dripping water.
First sip: a jounce,
an act of recognition;
third: an epiphany.
"These things can be forgotten,"
he assures me.

I think of that boy from long ago,
the spark of his morning eyes.
The desire I turned into a ghost—
and yet.
He's forever a comma, wedged
into the mud of a sentence.

When You Were a Girl

Always, you had a lineup in your head,
a twitching landscape of knees and shoulders
in varying shades.
You picked out new models
from the catalog of the world;
basted them with your eyes,
practicing their kinesics,
co-opting their twangs,
the casual turns of their wrists,
the crossings of their thighs—
their profanities.
As you sponged these affectations,
you hovered about yourself
like an indifferent lover,
working away, determinedly.

A day came when you believed
you'd managed to exit yourself;
your body was a vehicle.
Leaving the flashers on,
you'd parked it in the break-down lane.

You're a grown-up, now,
and in your closet, there are:
fine-knit scarves for the Park Avenue
winter caroling
that Anna never misses;
a paisley-patterned tunic
suited for Priscilla,
for the St. Barth's vacation
she takes every March;
a gray cocktail dress constructed
with spiderwebs of tulle—
you bought it because it looks
as fragile as a winter breath,
and in it, dead Laure would've been a vision.

Suspended in the corners, there are
four nubby-fabricked pencil skirts
marked with holes from
your daze of corporate misery;
an inches-thick wool sweater
that held you in place,
during a kiss with a skim-milk-pale,
whiskered man;
and the most odious item,
a sapphire-blue bolero commissioned
for a stillborn wedding.
The stitches split against the hanger,
as if, they, too, could never decide
about the veracity of your lives.

Ship of Theseus

Who was the girl who loved you, once, twenty years gone to the past? I declared myself a statue, then. Did you know I was the cast?

Some vestiges persist today, that rattlesnake of a snore. Only true oddities find themselves elected thus: traits most likely to endure.

Tectonic shifts have come inside; an organ has been plundered. Two children stacked their spines within, pressing hipbone gates asunder.

Can I calculate the balance of what's been bartered, what's been gained? A father swapped out for a son; a brother, gone, estranged.

I've lost so much, and readily; persons, places, times. I can no longer say with certainty, what I mean by *me* or *mine.*

Teaching My Husband How to Die

For thirty-two years,
we've marked each other,
doubling our body points.
Paired hips became butterflies;
linked hands, boulders.
We were moss growing
on each other's stones.
I've found myself seasoned with him
as I shopped for seedless
raspberry jam or shaved my legs at the gym.
Someone would need to scrape us
from each other with a broken-off twig,
to achieve a lasting separation,
I laughed once.
The sound echoed
with bravado.

Now the Florida air shakes
raindrops and insects
through its sieve
while a minister sanctifies his soul.
A hospice nurse appears,
flushing morphine
into the blue river of his vein.
"Don't hold on, only for me.
You go when you have to,"
I force my tongue to lie.

I blink now at his still-breathing remains:
the man-sized envelope of skin,
too thin to bear weight beyond its own.
It wheezes.
My fingers waver in the air,
but caresses in these final days
have brutalized him—
causing the quail's eggs to roll
under the lids.
We'll never touch again.

My Son Is Twelve

When my son was born, I wore a necklace with three charms that jingled as they skipped back and forth along the chain. Birdsong became my-song, siphoned from the branches of the mulberry tree that sits, watchful, in our yard. When he became a toddler, my son's grappling hands threatened to transform my prize into a golden noose. I put it away into a carved box.

I forgot about it, until I was cleaning out a bathroom drawer, removing strata of wasted hairs and opaque fingernail moons. The necklace had become thick with knots. I laid it upon the travertine counter, prying into the tiny pursed mouths with a sewing needle while remaining careful not to break the links.

After many tries, the chain slackened. I restored it to the round of my neck; I could do this, for the danger had passed. There's no one who yanks me down to him—urgently—enjoining me to drink from the spring water of his skin. I started to move, carrying myself from room to room. The sound was throatier now, no longer gay and breathless.

The Dauphine

Every chair my eight-year-old daughter sits upon scrambles to remake itself into a throne. Afternoons, she queens about our yard, elbows and ankles transmitting coded flashes at the sun. *No*, you *come* here.

She issues proclamations and verdicts, inscribed on parchment with blood-red crayon. My latest selection of vitamins pleases her, nearly as much as Skittles—*and Skittles are our all-time favorites.*

She's compiled a list of enemies, from amongst her subjects in the third grade. The entry, once made, is irreversible. I protest; I become my own echo; I grow hoarse.

Other parents cock their heads to the side, when I introduce myself as her mother. "Oh, we've heard all about *her*," they say. "She just needs more structure," others tell me, experts all. I'd like to drink from their fountains of confidence.

But at dinner two nights back, she placed a burning hand upon mine, leaning in as if she needed me. Shrinking her lips to a flame, she proffered a kiss; her whole being contracted into the shape of a child.

Jessica McEntee is an instructor at Westport Writers' Workshop in Connecticut whose work has appeared in *Ragazine, The Write Launch* and *Wingless Dreamer*. She won an Honorable Mention in the Third Wednesday 2019 Poetry Contest. Her web site is jessicamcentee.com. A magna cum laude graduate of Amherst College, she served as a fiction reader for the College's literary magazine, *The Common*, and writes reviews for BookTrib.com.

CPSIA information can be obtained
at www.ICGtesting.com
Printed in the USA
BVHW030211220619
551703BV00001B/9/P